365
First Line Writing Prompts

By Adrienne M. Clark

Adrienne M. Clark

365 First Line Writing Prompts

Copyright © Adrienne M. Clark
Published: November 2014
ISBN-13: 978-1503174740
ISBN-10: 1503174743
Publisher: Drakko Elements Publishing
www.drakkoelements.wix.com/drakkoelements

All rights reserved. No part of this publication may be reproduced, stored in retrieval system, copied in any form or by any means, electronic, mechanical, photocopying, recording or otherwise transmitted without written permission from the publisher. You must not circulate this book in any format.

drakkoelementspublishing@gmail.com

The writer claims no bearing on work you have written using the provided sentences.

Adrienne M. Clark

Table of Contents

Table of Contents 5
Dedication 7
Introduction... 9
How to Use... 11
The Prompts..17
Conclusion..62
About the Author..63
Author Contact Info 64
Other Works by Author 65
Books by Drakko Elements Publishing................66
Notes 67
Notes 68

Adrienne M. Clark

365 First Line Writing Prompts

Dedication

I dedicate this book to my little brother Adam Clark who never got to see me fulfill my dream of publishing. Thank you for all the encouragement over the years. You always had my back when my doubts tried to consume me. When nobody else cared if I followed my dream, you did. I love you wherever you are. I know you still have my back and you're still chirping in my ear to keep writing.

Adrienne M. Clark

365 First Line Writing Prompts

Introduction

This book was created with writers in mind but could also work for anyone looking for a mental pick-me-up.

It can be used as a break from a larger writing project, an exercise or just for fun. Entirely up to you how you use it. It could even be used by someone needing a little inspiration or just looking for something different to write. I provide you with a sentence and you do your magic with it.

Adrienne M. Clark

365 First Line Writing Prompts

How to Use

There are multiple options but the main one is to use the provided prompt for the start of a paragraph, short story, or any other size of fictional work. It could even be the first line of your next novel.

An alternate to try is change up the punctuation. Keep the words the same and in the same order but change all the rest. Turn it into multiple sentences or add more to it. Do whatever you like, as long as the words stay in the same order.

Example using the first line:

"Halt! No man shall pass, only the woman."

Could become:

"Halt. No. Man shall pass only. The woman is mine."

See how the meaning has changed?

Another bit you can play with is the slang or spelling.

Example:

no to nah **or** running to runnin'

Basically play with it and exercise your mind.

I'm only providing the words; the rest is up to you. Some of you may be wondering why I didn't simply leave out all punctuation and just leave behind words?

There are multiple reasons I didn't do that. One is not everyone's brains work the same. Some people don't have the skills to fill in their own punctuation or understand the words without them as guides. There's nothing wrong with that. Another reason is the challenge. Can you look past what is already there and turn it into something new? If not, no harm, no foul; but if you can, awesome.

Next question, how many times can you do it? How many times can you give the same words different content or meaning?

Example:

"Halt! No man shall pass; only the woman."

"Halt. No. Man shall pass only. The woman is mine."

"Halt. No man shall pass. Only the woman."

"Halt. No man shall. Pass only. The woman is right."

See how the meaning has changed but the words remain the same? Personally I don't like the sound of the fourth example but that's just my personal opinion. It feels too choppy for me but if it inspires you to write more than it's done its job well.

If you really want to challenge yourself then try writing at least one paragraph or page for

Adrienne M. Clark

every prompt. It's a good way to get the creative mind turning.

Overall I don't want to tell you what you have to do with this book. I just want to give you a guide you can choose to follow or you can break away and use this any way you please.

I do suggest you at least try to set a time minimum and stick to it. Even if you don't write anything, if you at least try to keep thinking you're still being productive. After all, your mind is your most important tool when it comes to writing.

So now I hand the control over to you. Write on and have fun.

365 First Line Writing Prompts

Adrienne M. Clark

The Prompts

1. "Halt! No man shall pass, only the woman."

2. It was the last day she'd ever see.

3. Two songs grated against one another.

4. "Don't mind her, she's a bit of a loon."

5. "The wax stings for but a second."

6. "I didn't say you could move."

7. "Why don't you go around the back?"

8. "Don't worry, I only bite hard, never through."

9. The bulge in his pants drew more attention than she wanted to give."

10. When she woke she felt pressure on her chest.

11. The empty gnawing pain radiated from his stomach.

12. "Ah crap, this is not how I wanted to die."

13. "You think you can come in here a little girl?"

14. The trigger cocking was all I heard.

15. Today like every other day, sucks.

16. "What was I supposed to do, it's not like I had a choice?"

17. "Please don't do this."

18. "Don't ever ask me to do that again."

19. This wasn't exactly how I saw my life turning out.

20. "What are you going to tell her?"

21. "You expect me to believe that?"

22. "The sex was amazing, but..."

23. "We're running out of time."

24. "Don't look at me."

25. "Don't give me that look, you know what you did."

26. "I wasn't gonna say anything, but..."

27. "Ah crap, I did it again."

28. "What do you say we get out of here?"

29. "Well I didn't expect to see that."

30. "What was your name again?"

31. "Your tardiness is going to cost you."

32. "I can't believe you would do that to someone."

33. "Just because it feels right, doesn't mean it is."

34. "I'll save you."

35. "Do you want me to rip your tongue out?"

36. One more minute.

37. It crept closer and closer.

38. There is no hope.

39. She could feel every agonizing second.

40. It isn't always gonna be this way.

41. She just watched it spin around and around.

42. "What are you supposed to say to that?"

43. The time was right but he was not.

44. "I'm not gonna tell you again!"

45. It's not like it's the end of the world.

46. "What do you want from me?"

47. "Are we there yet?"

48. He watched her tongue dart out.

49. "No, no, a million times no!"

50. The change was subtle.

51. It couldn't get much worse.

52. All she wanted to do was pull the hair out.

53. She awoke to her heart trying to beat out of her chest.

54. It wasn't the first time and it wouldn't be the last.

55. "Don't know what to expect, but..."

56. "It wasn't like I was gonna tell."

57. The past isn't always the best place to start.

58. "I know I need to pull myself together."

59. Those who can't do, teach.

60. It's not like I wanted to hurt anyone.

61. It's not going to help.

62. After all this we're in it together.

63. "Don't stop."

64. She watched it descend on her.

65. "You know I love you, right?"

66. She watched as it closed in on her.

67. The clouds moved in so quickly she didn't know what to do.

68. It's not like she'd ever done it before.

69. The light grew brighter as it got closer.

70. That isn't what I meant.

71. "I just don't see how I can help you."

72. I never knew I had a sister.

73. "Hands against the wall and spread."

74. "Don't step on that."

75. It was the last thing I expected to hear.

76. Despite what she thought, my sacrifice had nothing to do with her.

77. It's not everyday you roll over to find yourself dead.

78. When I looked in the mirror I could barely contain my scream.

79. "You can't ask this of me."

80. The warrior within was ready to come out.

81. Despite how soft her fur was, I was still reluctant to touch it.

82. It's not every day you get to meet your idol.

83. I could feel them crawling over me.

84. When I touched it I was absorbed, like I'd become one with it.

85. I could hear her whimpering across the room.

86. "You can't ask me to stay and then force me to go!"

87. One arm in, my head partially through and I was stuck.

88. I clenched my fists to hide the tremble.

89. It's not everyday you watch your life flash before your eyes.

90. "It's not like I wanna be famous, just rich."

91. "You'll see me again!"

92. One hundred inventive ways to die.

93. I thought my heart stopped.

94. Everywhere I looked was this shimmering light that consumed me.

95. My best dream morphed into my worst nightmare in the span of a few seconds.

96. Blood is not what you wanna see first thing upon waking.

97. "Ever heard of a vampire afraid of blood?"

98. Too bad it wasn't my worst decision.

99. Which way to turn?

100. They said I'd be sorry.

101. "Take a trip with me to the past."

102. If you knew the day you were created when you were going to die, what would you do?"

103. It's not like I asked to be born different.

104. I wasn't given any choice.

105. As the ground approached I could do nothing to stop it.

106. I saw it coming but was helpless to avoid it.

107. I'll give him this, he was a handsome boy.

108. I just wish he hadn't been bat crap crazy.

109. I saw her once in a dream.

110. The reality was so much better.

111. "What, you expect me to die, for you?"

112. "You're not worth the ground I walk on."

113. He hid in the shadows.

114. She wasted precious seconds watching the moon rise.

115. "Did I ever tell you how much I hate heights?"

116. "I apologize now if I crap myself."

117. It's not like I meant to do it.

118. What's one more genius in a world full of rejects?

119. Her eyes were seared shut.

120. All he could find was one pink sock and one blue.

121. It's never better at the beginning.

122. His palm itched to slap her.

123. Some people don't get how stupid they really are.

124. "For a genius you're pretty daft."

125. "I never claimed I was smart, just smarter than you."

126. The ground trembled upon its approach.

127. "Hiding under a desk won't help."

128. "If you're as smart as you think you are, you'll be able to get out of this."

129. Their butts were just asking for a spanking.

130. The bed looked inviting, she did not.

131. "What's one more year?"

132. "If you can dish it, I can take it."

133. "That's an awful long time to live in exile."

134. "You think you can do better?"

135. "I'm gonna kill her."

136. The risks involved were just too high.

137. She never stood a chance.

138. He didn't know where he was going.

139. She was the death of me once.

140. "Don't stop!"

141. "Can't wait to get my hands on you."

142. Tick, tock, goes the clock.

143. "You're in trouble now."

144. "If I were you, I'd run."

145. My stomach heaved.

146. It's not every day you get to kiss a princess.

147. It was such a terrible beauty.

148. Everything seemed to go in slow motion.

149. Beware the rising storm.

150. There are worse things than death.

151. Passion is all I feel.

152. "Don't tempt me."

153. The end was merely the beginning.

154. "If you had to do it all over again..."

155. "Don't tell me you like it."

156. "Keep your mouth shut and let me..."

157. "Is everything a game to you?"

158. There were way too many potential hiding places.

159. It looked like the shadows were going to jump out and bite.

160. She started out sucking before clamping down hard.

161. The illusion of life is not mine.

162. "I can't believe I died yesterday."

163. "What's it like being dead?"

164. It's not everyday I shake hands with a corpse.

165. "If you wanted to scare me, you're doing a great job."

166. "I think I'll be leaving now."

167. "Would you care to dance?"

168. His bow was as formal as his posture was stiff.

169. "I told you we went the wrong way."

170. "Please, don't start."

171. This is how it always goes.

172. One step in and the other way out.

173. Too many dirty socks.

174. She grimaced in the mirror while picking trash out of her hair.

175. The last thing I saw before hitting the floor, was blood caked boots.

176. "This isn't exactly where I want to be either."

177. The thud, thud, thud was enough to drive anyone insane.

365 First Line Writing Prompts

178. "If you're ready to listen, then I'm ready to tell."

179. Pink is the last colour I want to see.

180. "Please tell me there's another way out."

181. "About that, sorry."

182. Here we go again.

183. Every book fell off the shelf.

184. It's not every day you get to taste ambrosia.

185. I could still taste him on my lips.

186. She has no idea how much damage she does.

187. If only there was a way.

188. Too much, it's all too much.

189. It's everywhere I look, everything I see.

190. It looked like any other stone house.

191. One by one they all disappeared.

192. It was somewhere between a flurry and a storm.

193. I couldn't hide from the pitter patter of little feet.

365 First Line Writing Prompts

194. "I don't know what I'm supposed to do now."

195. "They told me you'd be here!"

196. "Give me your hand."

197. Should I stay or should I jump?

198. Don't tease him.

199. Time is running out.

200. It wasn't the best time to venture out on my own.

201. It was getting precariously close to her fingers.

202. "Oh man, I just bought that."

203. Ever ask yourself why you do what you do?

204. I guess I should have thought about my actions before following through.

205. "Do you think one box will be enough?"

206. "One dead cat wasn't enough, you had to go with ten."

207. "If I asked you to scream, would you?"

208. "Not again."

209. I didn't think it could get much worse.

210. I was tempted.

211. "Oh don't start that again."

212. "Did you really expect me to buy that?"

213. "I know you're stupid but come on."

214. "I'm glad I'm not in your shoes."

215. "Don't turn around."

216. "Ever see a dog humping a monkey?"

217. "I guess I'm just that one in thirty thousand."

218. "Just keep on walking."

219. "No loitering."

220. "Now what do you want?"

221. "There's the door."

222. "I was fine before you showed up."

223. "Damn it's cold in here."

224. "Hide under the blankets."

225. As I watched her pull out of the driveway it dawned on me that she was serious.

226. My heart is in a million pieces.

365 First Line Writing Prompts

227. Oh no, I've had enough of this.

228. I watch as the bus flies by.

229. The door was stuck.

230. I thought I was doing good.

231. What a mess.

232. I guess I'll never know.

233. Toothpicks in cocktail weenies.

234. It was the button to end it all, and her thump was poised and ready.

235. It wasn't one of my better moves.

236. I heard it tear.

237. "Quick, hit the lights."

238. "Don't say I never gave you anything."

239. Ever wanted to rip out your own eyeball?

240. "I thought you said he was dead."

241. "I didn't know it could do that."

242. "And I thought I was bad."

243. "Does it smell in here?"

244. "I told you I was having a bad day!"

245. She felt nothing as she stared down the barrel of the gun.

246. It wasn't every day that someone magically appeared in front of you.

247. No matter how hard he looked he couldn't find a pen.

248. When I turned on the tap I was expecting water.

249. The wolf jumped out of the picture.

250. Her mouth was open as if to scream but no sound came out.

251. "If I didn't know any better I'd say you're mean."

252. Just because I'm pretty doesn't mean I have a brain.

253. I'm about as stereotypical as you get.

254. They didn't tell me it was going to be like this.

255. Just when I thought it was safe to stop, I heard him behind me.

256. In one fell swoop everything came crashing down.

257. It wasn't like I was using that hand.

258. "If you don't believe me then ask her yourself."

365 First Line Writing Prompts

259. "Not in your life."

260. "Some people would say I'm crazy, those people would be right."

261. I only took a little.

262. I was so hungry.

263. I thought I loved him more than I loved myself, until I was put to the test.

264. I wasn't expecting her tail to snap off.

265. I was able to breathe much easier after he was done.

266. I didn't know it would turn out like this.

267. "Who do you think you are?"

268. "Just get out of my sight."

269. "Get off my site!"

270. "I never said you could be here."

271. I watched it fall and there was nothing I could do to stop it.

272. "How did you get this number?"

273. It's not like I meant to kill her.

274. "The truth is I have no idea what I'm doing."

275. "No it doesn't go in there."

365 First Line Writing Prompts

276. "I can't do this without you."

277. "I didn't mean for this to happen."

278. "Oh great, look who's coming."

279. "Careful, I bite."

280. "Before you jump to conclusions..."

281. "I knew I'd see you again."

282. I wasn't sure what to think when he rounded the corner.

283. As he slid towards me I braced for impact.

284. "I'm not sure what you see in him."

285. "Why do you want it?"

286. "I'm not ready to give it up."

287. Just like that, he was gone.

288. "I can't believe he's dead."

289. Reduced to nothing more than ashes.

290. I sat and watched my life.

291. Time to get going.

292. "I met you once, a long time ago."

293. I stared down the barrel so long everything else ceased to exist.

365 First Line Writing Prompts

294. I was minding my own business.

295. It doesn't take long.

296. Figures it would be him.

297. "Ouch, that hurt."

298. "Do you want to try the other hand?"

299. Her smiling face reminded me of a shrivelled up prune.

300. Everything started to fall.

301. I don't know how much I can take.

302. I just need one more.

303. The rumble was enough to startle everyone in the room.

304. "Don't ask me again, I won't tell you."

305. I knew there was trouble the second she walked in the door.

306. Bad doesn't even begin to explain.

307. "Why won't you just leave me alone?"

308. Blood was not what I wanted to see.

309. "I said I'd help you and I will."

310. "Is it getting cold in here?"

311. The temperature dropped ten degrees.

312. I couldn't focus.

313. It's not like I started out wanting to be a loser.

314. He moved away before I could stop him.

315. Some things just can't be undone.

316. "You can't have the day off."

317. "Stop or I'll shoot."

318. When I flipped open the book...

319. Too many children.

320. If I could just get my feet free...

321. Everywhere I looked, purple.

322. She'd been lost.

323. "Too bad it wasn't him instead."

324. What are you gonna do with one hand?

325. "I never agreed to this."

326. Anyone can do it.

327. "Please don't hurt me!"

328. "Naughty, naughty little girl."

329. "Is it time for your punishment?"

365 First Line Writing Prompts

330. "It normally takes two people."

331. I broke another.

332. "Don't tell me you believe."

333. "You like him, don't you?"

334. Angels are real.

335. I don't know how to stop.

336. She watched it bounce all the way to the ground.

337. "I'm not bad."

338. I might be a little evil.

339. "What am I supposed to do with you?"

340. "I tried to warn you."

341. "Why won't anyone listen to me?"

342. "I already told you this."

343. She watched as everything came crashing towards her.

344. "You're a pig."

345. "I know you are but what am I?"

346. Her arms felt weighed down with lead.

365 First Line Writing Prompts

347. Not everyday you get to kick a dinosaur.

348. "He went that way!"

349. Everything went silent.

350. "I told you he wasn't going to be any help."

351. "You just had to try it your way."

352. It crumpled way too easily.

353. "Are you sure?"

354. "Get off that!"

355. "I didn't say no so you could go ahead and do it anyway."

356. "I'll never help you."

357. "I'm standing right behind you."

358. "If you do, you die."

359. "Don't make the mistake of underestimating me."

360. "You're not gonna like how this turns out."

361. "Believe me when I tell you..."

362. "You think you can crap in my sandbox and I'm just gonna take it?"

365 First Line Writing Prompts

363. "I'd love to see you try."

364. Her claws splayed as they descended towards my face.

365. "I'm not sure if this is your usual technique but I'm really enjoying it."

Adrienne M. Clark

Conclusion

So now you've reached the end. I hope this was able to help you with your writing endeavours.

My only advice to you now is to just keep writing…no matter what. I'm not saying give up everything in your life to write but simply that you never stop. Write anything. Write out lists, brainstorm, poetry, ideas, stories, novels, blogs, anything. Just keep writing.

So now I'll let you do whatever it is you're going to do. Just remember, have fun. If it stops being fun, you're probably not trying hard enough, or you're trying too hard. Sure writing's hard, but you have to enjoy it or you wouldn't keep doing it.

About the Author

Adrienne M. Clark lives in a small town in Ontario, Canada with her spouse, daughters, cats and dog (despite allergies to the animals).

Writing has been a passion of hers since she started writing notes to a boy she liked when she was in grade seven. Years later and many twists and turns in the road and she is back with that boy, now a man and father of her children. Without his initial inspiration she never would have discovered her love of words.

Her favourite writing is fiction but she does it more for herself than for anyone else. However she feels the need to share the love of writing with others any way she can.

Adrienne M. Clark

Author Contact Info

If you want to contact her check out

Goodreads
http://www.goodreads.com/author/show/7481134.Adrienne_M_Clark

Facebook Author page
http://www.facebook.com/pages/Adrienne-M-Clark/345322165612061

Twitter
http://twitter.com/rosespike84

Other Works by Author

Improv Yourself
by Adrienne Clark
- March 2014
ISBN: 1496196104
ISBN-13: 978-1496196101
ASIN: B00IX587ZO
Are you a writer looking to exercise your mind? Look no further.
This book will show you a new way to look at words and sentences. Take the norm and twist it into something different. If you find yourself needing a break from a larger project or you just want to try something new then this book is for you.
How unique is your way of thinking? This book will put it to the test.

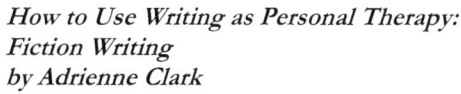

How to Use Writing as Personal Therapy: Fiction Writing
by Adrienne Clark
- March 2014
ISBN: 1597466415
ISBN-13: 978-1497466418
ASIN: B00JARBO9A
Do you prefer to help yourself work through issues? Try fiction writing as a therapy technique today!
Instead of spending an arm and a leg, or two, on therapy bills have you ever considered writing as a vent for your inner turmoil? It may not work for everyone but you could be surprised at what it can do for you. If you already enjoy writing then maybe this is the perfect outlet waiting to be found.

Adrienne M. Clark

Books by Drakko Elements Publishing

Soaring Hearts
180 page Sketchbook Journal

Original and Altered Artwork by Adrienne M. Clark

ISBN: 1507643950
ISBN-13: 978-1507643952

Window to the Soul
180 page Sketchbook Journal

Original and Altered Photo By Adrienne M. Clark

ISBN: 1507505035
ISBN-13: 978-1507505037

Wind Singer
180 page Sketchbook Journal

Original Artwork by Blair Hill Altered by Adrienne M. Clark

ISBN: 1507690215
ISBN-13: 978-1507690215

365 First Line Writing Prompts

Notes

Adrienne M. Clark

Notes

Printed in Great Britain
by Amazon.co.uk, Ltd.,
Marston Gate.